ADVICE AND CONSENT

ADVICE AND CONSENT

A Play in One Act

YXTA MAYA MURRAY

Introduction & Score by

KATHLEEN KIM

This is a LARB Provocations publication
Published by The Los Angeles Review of Books
6671 Sunset Blvd., Suite 1521, Los Angeles, CA 90028
www.larbbooks.org

Cover artwork: Yxta Maya Murray, Untitled (2010)

ISBN 978-1-940660-50-9

Library of Congress Control Number 2018965699

Contents

Introduction

Kathleen Kim

WHEN MY COLLEAGUE Yxta Maya Murray invited me to collaborate with her on this project, I was ambivalent. Brett Kavanaugh's Senate confirmation left me in a condition of devastated paralysis. The confirmation process displayed a patronizing disregard for Christine Blasey Ford's convincing and familiar testimony of sexual assault. It also reaped gratuitous sympathy for Kavanaugh, a straight white male Yale Law School graduate who appealed to his top grades, indignant love of beer and sports, and partisan hatred to justify his appointment to the highest court. The brazen spectacle of systemic domination of women, people of color, and other minorities by our justice system invoked a profound sense of helplessness for me and many others. The Constitution failed to protect the integrity of the Supreme Court, which, until that point, remained as the only hopeful check on abuse of political power.

Yxta is an influential legal scholar and writer, whose creative output is wide-ranging and impactful. Her legal writing details her immersion in communities displaced and blighted by poverty and natural disaster to advance modern-day understanding of property rights. She examines the expression of abstract artists as a commentary on access to justice for survivors of domestic violence. She is also an award-winning novelist, whose fiction channels fantasy to uncover the weight of reality. My writing draws from frontline experience defending immigrants against governmental abuse to expose the power structures entrenched in our democracy. I compose and perform experimental music to expand the creative and conceptual process, incorporating sound as an abstraction of lived experience.

As legal scholars, Yxta and I share a critical approach to legal theory and its application: how the law in oblique and overt ways can fail to protect those most vulnerable and injure those already at the margins. Like other legal scholars, we turn to the Constitution as a source for critique as well as inspiration for interpretations that reveal its evolutive qualities.

The Bill of Rights, which sets forth individual fundamental rights such has freedom of speech, freedom from discrimination, and constitutional due process, has extended protection to historically oppressed groups against invidious, discriminatory governmental action. The Supreme Court — as the final arbiter of the scope of fundamental rights — has at times interpreted the Constitution progressively, to ensure reproductive freedom, marital and sexual relations with whomever one chooses, freedom from enslavement in all its forms, and freedom from discrimination on the basis of race, gender, religion, and alienage.

Kavanaugh's confirmation to the Supreme Court corrodes basic constitutional principles that have been relied upon to preserve liberal democracy. Although federal judges are appointed by elected officials, they must also demonstrate nonpartisanship and moral integrity through a rigorous Senate confirmation process that interrogates their character — this is especially true for Supreme Court nominees. The independence of the federal judiciary preserves the separation of powers and ensures that countermajoritarian concerns are heard when the political branches pursue only the policy preferences of their electorate. Under the Trump regime, our imperiled democracy is in danger of extinction.

This threat to democratic freedom would likely trigger a fight or flight response in those who sense imminent jeopardy to justice and survival. Yet, for legal scholars amidst a constitutional crisis, the enormity of this threat is immobilizing; it can neither be overpowered nor escaped. The alarming absence of legal tools to grapple with the threat prompts an emotional, physical, and cognitive paralysis. Activating this stasis requires a radical departure from jurisprudence and an approach to critical legal theory that is novel and multi-disciplinary. With this project, *Advice and Consent: A Play in One Act*, Yxta and I offer such a method, a creative space where law intersects with art in the form of dramatic theater accompanied by a musical score.

Advice and Consent is a play that captures the legal drama that ensued during the Kavanaugh hearings by using actual testimony from Blasey Ford, Kavanaugh, Senators Flake and Collins, as well as perspectives from anonymous characters and others. By framing the testimony as a dialogue between the characters, the play engages in a skillful study of contrasts raising issues about power, privilege, domination, misogyny, and racism. For example, during the actual confirmation hearings Blasey Ford's testimony was followed by Kavanaugh's testimony; this arbitrary order all but erased the force of Blasey Ford's initial presentation, and facilitated the dominance of Kavanaugh's silencing rage.

Advice and Consent deconstructs the capricious structuring of the confirmation process to reveal the complexities in the deeply problematic statements and disturbing responses that the confirmation process elicited. Anonymous characters with diverse ideological and demographic backgrounds share perspectives that are both familiar and surprising. Their identity politics inform their reactions to the confirmation hearings, which the observer may find relatable, but also incendiary.

Inspired by Yxta's assemblage, I composed the musical score to include a total of nine players: at least five of whom are women and/or LGBTQ+ and at least four of whom are people of color. The nine players represent an imagined Supreme Court where diversity, while perhaps token, matters for justice and progressivism. Avant jazz, improvisation and protest music inform important aspects of the score. Although these genres have traditionally been dominated by male musicians, they defied former conventions and often served as mobilizing forces for social justice movements. The score attempts to access the legacy of resistance that these musical forms carry.

I am grateful to Yxta for the opportunity to contribute to this project as both a legal scholar and composer. Blending these creative roles enables me to engage with and confront the present-day extremes of injustice rather than withdraw from them.

Preface

Yxta Maya Murray

ON SEPTEMBER 27, 2018, the Senate Judiciary Committee held hearings concerning Dr. Christine Blasey Ford's allegations that then-Supreme Court Justice nominee Judge Brett Kavanaugh had sexually assaulted her in the mid-1980s.[1] Dr. Blasey Ford gave her testimony first, and Judge Kavanaugh, who sat on the Court of Appeals for the District of Columbia Circuit, followed.

Nine days later, on October 6, the Senate voted to confirm Justice Kavanaugh in a 50-48 vote.[2] It did so in dispatch of its duties articulated in Article II, Section 2 of the U.S. Constitution, which empowers the Senate to give the President of the United States advice and consent in the appointment of federal judges.[3]

This play is formed out of interviews I have conducted with women and men about the accusations, hearings, and confirmation of Justice Kavanaugh. I also created it from found text,[4] name-

---

1   Sheryl Gay Stolberg and Nicholas Fandos, *Brett Kavanaugh and Christine Blasey Ford Duel With Tears and Fury,* N.Y. TIMES, Sept. 27, 2018, https://www.nytimes.com/2018/09/27/us/politics/brett-kavanaugh-confirmation-hearings.html.

2   Annie Daniel, Jasmine C. Lee and Sara Simon, *How Every Senator Voted on Kavanaugh's Confirmation,* N.Y. TIMES, Oct. 6, 2018, https://www.nytimes.com/interactive/2018/10/06/us/politics/kavanaugh-live-vote-senate-confirmation.html.

3   *See* US Const. art II, § 2, cl. 2 "([The President] shall have Power,...[to] nominate, and by and with the Advice and Consent of the Senate, shall appoint Ambassadors, other public Ministers and Consuls, Judges of the supreme Court, and all other Officers of the United States, whose Appointments are not herein otherwise provided for, and which shall be established by Law: but the Congress may by Law vest the Appointment of such inferior Officers, as they think proper, in the President alone, in the Courts of Law, or in the Heads of Departments.").

4   *See, cf.,* M. Perloff, *Found Poetry,* in THE PRINCETON ENCYCLOPEDIA OF POETRY AND POETICS 503 (2012) ("Found poetry, also called the poetry of citation or appropriation, is

ly, transcripts of the September 27 hearing,[5] of protesters arguing with Senator Jeff Flake (R-AZ) in the moments before the September 28 Senate Judiciary Committee vote on whether to let Kavanaugh's nomination proceed to the full Senate,[6] and of Senator Susan Collins's (R-ME) October 5 explanation for why she would vote yes on Kavanaugh the next day.[7]

Inspired by the pathbreaking work by Anna Deavere Smith, I rearrange, select, and edit the testimony of both Dr. Blasey Ford and Judge Kavanaugh for poetic and provocative effect. I also arrange, select, and edit the other texts. In some cases, I have combined interviews into one monologue. I often quote the transcripts and interviews verbatim, which creates an occasional roughness in the dialogues and monologues that reveal the intensity of the speakers' emotions.

I designed this drama as a thought experiment about power, pathos, tragedy, politics, gender, race, and truth. Accompanied by a score written by law professor and violinist Kathleen Kim, it may be either read or performed.

---

created by taking words, phrases, and, even more commonly, entire passages from other sources and reframing them as 'poetry' by altering the context, frame, and format in which the source text appears.'").

5   *Kavanaugh Hearing Transcript*, THE WASH. POST, Sept. 27, 2018, https://www.washingtonpost.com/news/national/wp/2018/09/27/kavanaugh-hearing-transcript/?utm_term=.0dcd27227760.

6   *See* Niraj Chokshi and Astead W. Herndon, *Jeff Flake Is Confronted on Video By Sexual Assault Survivors,* Sept. 28, N.Y. TIMES, 2018, https://www.nytimes.com/2018/09/28/us/politics/jeff-flake-protesters-kavanaugh.html.

7   *Read Susan Collins's Speech Declaring Support for Brett Kavanaugh,* N.Y. TIMES, Oct. 5, 2018, https://www.nytimes.com/2018/10/05/us/politics/susan-collins-speech-brett-kavanaugh.html

ADVICE AND CONSENT

SCRIPT

Characters

Dr. Christine Blasey Ford
Judge Brett Kavanaugh
Anonymous 1
Anonymous 2
Anonymous 3
Anonymous 4
Maria Gallagher
Ana Maria Archila
Senator Jeff Flake (R-AZ)
Senator Susan Collins (R-ME)

Time

September 27, 2018, 10:00 a.m.-6:45 p.m., EST, and its aftermath.

Places

The Senate Chamber in the United States Capitol.
A nondescript room.

SCENE ONE

No curtain. No scenery. The stage is set with 10 chairs. DR. CHRISTINE BLASEY FORD sits in one chair, and JUDGE BRETT KAVANAUGH sits in a chair beside her. BLASEY FORD and KAVANAUGH face a panel of eight seated players: ANONYMOUS 1, ANONYMOUS 2, ANONYMOUS 3, ANONYMOUS 4, SENATOR JEFF FLAKE (R-AZ), MARIA GALLAGHER, ANA MARIA ARCHILA, and SENATOR SUSAN COLLINS (R-ME).

Score plays.

BLASEY FORD and KAVANAUGH look at each other, and then look away. They look at the rest of the players but seem aware of each other.

Score stops.

BLASEY FORD

I'll lean forward. Is this good?[8]

KAVANAUGH

Thank you for allowing me to make my statement. I wrote it myself yesterday afternoon and evening. No one has seen a draft, or it, except for one of my former law clerks. This is my statement.

BLASEY FORD

My name is Christine Blasey Ford. I am a professor of psychology at Palo Alto University and a research psychologist at the Stanford

---

8   This text has been selected and rearranged by the author from the transcript provided by THE WASHINGTON POST, *see* note 5, *supra*.

University School of Medicine. I have been married to Russell Ford since 2002 and we have two children.

I am here today not because I want to be. I am terrified.

KAVANAUGH

People have been willing to do anything, to make any physical threat against my family —

BLASEY FORD

I am here because I believe it is my civic duty to tell you what happened to me while Brett Kavanaugh and I were in high school.

KAVANAUGH

(*cries loudly*)

[People have been willing] to send any violent e-mail to my wife, to make any kind of allegation against me and against my friends. To blow me up and take me down.

BLASEY FORD

We've relocated now twice.

KAVANAUGH

This is a circus.

BLASEY FORD

In the summer of 1982, like most summers, I spent most every day at the Columbia Country Club in Chevy Chase, Maryland, swimming and practicing diving.

One evening that summer, after a day of diving at the club, I attended a small gathering at a house in the Bethesda area. There were four boys I remember specifically being there: Brett

Kavanaugh, Mark Judge, a boy named P.J., and one other boy whose name I cannot recall. I also remember my friend Leland attending.

I do not remember all of the details of how that gathering came together, but like many that summer, it was almost surely a spur-of-the-moment gathering.

I truly wish I could be more helpful —

KAVANAUGH

This has destroyed my family and my good name. A good name built up through the decades of very hard work and public service at the highest levels of the American government.

BLASEY FORD

But the details that — about that night that bring me here today are the ones I will never forget. They have been seared into my memory, and have haunted me episodically as an adult.

KAVANAUGH

(to BLASEY FORD)

You sowed the wind for decades to come. I fear that the whole country will reap the whirlwind.

(BLASEY FORD looks frightened)

FLAKE

We'll take a five minute break now.

<u>SCENE TWO</u>

Score plays.

BLASEY FORD and KAVANAUGH lean back in their seats, breathing laboriously. ANONYMOUS 1 gets up out of her chair and exits, stage right. ANONYMOUS 4 gets up out of her chair and exits, stage left. ANONYMOUS 1 returns with a glass of water and gives it to KAVANAUGH. ANONYMOUS 4 returns with a cup of coffee and gives it to BLASEY FORD. BLASEY FORD smiles at Anonymous 4 in thanks, and otherwise performs her self-protective raced and gendered role at the hearings.

KAVANAUGH and BLASEY FORD drink. They give back their cups to ANONYMOUS 1 and ANONYMOUS 4, respectively. As BLASEY FORD returns her cup to ANONYMOUS 4, she smiles again. KAVANAUGH remains stern-faced.

ANONYMOUS 1 and ANONYMOUS 4 exit stage right and left, respectively. They return without the cups. They take their seats.

Score stops.

BLASEY FORD

When I got to the small gathering, people were drinking beer in a small living room/family room-type area on the first floor of the house. I drank one beer. Brett and Mark were visibly drunk.

KAVANAUGH

What goes around comes around. I am an optimistic guy.

BLASEY FORD

Early in the evening, I went up a very narrow set of stairs leading from the living room to a second floor to use the restroom. When I got to the top of the stairs, I was pushed from behind into a bedroom across from the bathroom. I couldn't see who pushed me. Brett and Mark came into the bedroom and locked the door behind them.

There was music playing in the bedroom. It was turned up louder by either Brett or Mark once we were in the room.

KAVANAUGH

I am innocent of this charge.

BLASEY FORD

I was pushed onto the bed, and Brett got on top of me. He began running his hands over my body and grinding into me. I yelled, hoping that someone downstairs might hear me, and I tried to get away from him, but his weight was heavy.

KAVANAUGH

I am innocent of this charge … I'm innocent … I'm — I'm innocent … I'm innocent … I'm innocent of this charge … I'm — I'm innocent.

BLASEY FORD

(cries softly)

Brett groped me and tried to take off my clothes. He had a hard time, because he was very inebriated —

KAVANAUGH

I drank beer with my friends. Almost everyone did. Sometimes I had too many beers. Sometimes others did. I liked beer. I still like beer. But I did not drink beer to the point of blacking out, and I never sexually assaulted anyone.

BLASEY FORD

He was very inebriated. I believed he was going to rape me.

I tried to yell for help. When I did, Brett put his hand over my mouth to stop me from yelling.

KAVANAUGH

There is a bright line between drinking beer, which I gladly do, and which I fully embrace, and sexually assaulting someone, which is a violent crime. If every American who drinks beer or every American who drank beer in high school is suddenly presumed guilty of sexual assault, [it] will be an ugly, new place in this country. I never committed sexual assault.

BLASEY FORD

This is what terrified me the most, and has had the most lasting impact on my life. It was hard for me to breathe, and I thought that Brett was accidentally going to kill me.

KAVANAUGH

Yes, we drank beer. My friends and I, the boys and girls. Yes, we drank beer. I liked beer. Still like beer. We drank beer. The drinking age, as I noted, was 18, so the seniors were legal, senior year in high school, people were legal to drink, and we — yeah, we drank beer, and I said sometimes — sometimes probably had too many beers, and sometimes other people had too many beers. We drank beer. We liked beer.

BLASEY FORD

I was too afraid and ashamed to tell anyone these details. I did not want to tell my parents that I, at age 15, was in a house without any parents present, drinking beer with boys.

KAVANAUGH

We drank beer, and you know, so — so did, I think, the vast majority of — of people our age at the time. But in any event, we drank beer, and — and still do. So whatever, you know.

BLASEY FORD

My husband recalls that I named my attacker as Brett Kavanaugh. After … [a couple's] May 2012 therapy session, I did my best to ignore the memories of the assault, because recounting them caused me to relive the experience, and caused panic and anxiety.

KAVANAUGH

I was at the top of my class academically, busted my butt in school. Captain of the varsity basketball team.

BLASEY FORD

This changed in early July 2018. I saw press reports stating that Brett Kavanaugh was on the shortlist of a list of very well-qualified Supreme Court nominees.

KAVANAUGH

Got in Yale College. When I got into Yale College, got into Yale Law School. Worked my tail off.

BLASEY FORD

I thought it was my civic duty to relay the information I had about Mr. Kavanaugh's conduct so that those considering his nomination would know about this assault.

KAVANAUGH

I like beer. I like beer. I don't know if you do … do you like beer … or not? What do you like to drink? … what do you like to drink?

BLASEY FORD

— I provided the names of Brett Kavanaugh and Mark Judge.

KAVANAUGH

[Mark] was a friend at Georgetown Prep, starting in ninth grade. He's a — someone we would — in our, you know, group of friends. … I haven't talked to him in a couple years.

BLASEY FORD

I did see Mark Judge once at the Potomac Village Safeway after the time of the attack. And it would be helpful with anyone's resources if …

KAVANAUGH

[Mark] — he's already provided sworn testimony to the committee. … Mark Judge was … I'll explain it if you let me.

BLASEY FORD

If we could find out —

KAVANAUGH

Mark Judge was a friend of ours in high school who developed a very serious drinking problem, an addiction problem that lasted decades and was very difficult for him to escape from.

And he nearly died. And then developed — then he had leukemia as well, on top of it…

So, you know, we can sit here … we can sit here and you like, make — make fun of some guy who has an addiction.

I don't think that really makes — is really good.

BLASEY FORD

If we could find out … when he worked there, then I could provide a more detailed timeline as to when the attack occurred.

KAVANAUGH

You'd have to ask him.

SUSAN COLLINS

We'll adjourn for 45 minutes — or, not adjourn. Recess for 45 minutes.

Score plays.

SCENE THREE

BLASEY FORD and KAVANAUGH stay seated in their chairs. They breathe audibly and roughly. They look at the seated players. They look at the audience. They look at each other, and then look away.

Score stops.

BLASEY FORD

Indelible in the hippocampus is the laughter, the laugh — the uproarious laughter between the two, and their having fun at my expense.

KAVANAUGH

Let me take a step back and explain high school. I was number one in the class.

BLASEY FORD

They were laughing with each other. I was, you know, underneath one of them while the two laughed, two friends —

   (she cries)

KAVANAUGH

I busted my butt in academics. I always tried to do the best I could. As I recall, I finished one in the class, first in — you know, freshman and junior year, right at the top with Steve Clark and Eddie (inaudible), we were always kind of in the mix.

I — I played sports.

BLASEY FORD

— two friends having a really good time with one another.

KAVANAUGH

I was captain of the varsity basketball team. I was wide receiver and defensive back on the football team. I ran track in the spring of '82 to try to get faster.

BLASEY FORD

I was 15 at the time.

KAVANAUGH

I got into Yale Law School.

BLASEY FORD

I think I described earlier a fairly disastrous first two years of undergraduate studies at University of North Carolina, where I was finally able to pull myself together.

KAVANAUGH

That's the number one law school in the country.

BLASEY FORD

And then, once coping with — with the immediate impacts, the short-term impacts, I experienced, like, longer-term impacts of anxiety and relationship challenges.

KAVANAUGH

Ashley has been a rock. I thank God every day for Ashley and my family … Explaining this to our daughters [Margaret and Liza] has been about the worst experience of our lives.

BLASEY FORD

(voice hoarse and cracking)

I'm — I'm now just catching up with you, sorry … I'm a little slower.

KAVANAUGH

I am not questioning that Dr. Ford may have been sexually assaulted by some person in some place at some time. But I have never done that to her or to anyone.

BLASEY FORD

[I am] 100 percent [certain.]

KAVANAUGH

Zero [doubt], I'm 100 percent certain. Not a scintilla; 100 percent certain.

BLASEY FORD

I'm sorry … I'm sorry … I'm sorry … I'm sorry … My mind is getting a little tired.

KAVANAUGH

I swear to God.

BLASEY FORD

Thank you.

Score plays.

BLASEY FORD and KAVANAUGH stand up and offer to shake hands with each of the players. ANONYMOUS 1 shakes hands with KAVANAUGH but refuses the hand of BLASEY FORD. MARIA GALLAGHER and ANA MARIA ARCHILA shake BLASEY FORD's hand but refuse KAVANAUGH's. ANONYMOUS 2 shakes both BLASEY FORD and KAVANAUGH'S hands. ANONYMOUS 3 and 4 shake BLASEY FORD's hand but not KAVANAUGH'S. JEFF FLAKE and SUSAN COLLINS shake both BLASEY FORD's and KAVANAUGH's hands. BLASEY FORD exits stage right, taking her chair. KAVANAUGH exits stage left, taking his.

<u>SCENE FOUR</u>

ANONYMOUS 1 stands up from her chair. She stands in the middle of the stage and faces the audience.

Score stops.

ANONYMOUS I

There are so many good reasons not to believe this person. I see the way you are looking at me when I say that and I'm not sure I want to get into it with you. But there are. For one thing, I was attacked, too. When I was a younger woman. I was attacked by a man that I knew through my mother. He — I don't want to get into it, but he did. And I told the police. He didn't, no, he didn't. He didn't go to jail. But I told the police and I made a record. And I believe that any woman who was truly attacked would do the same. It's a matter of honor. Also, it's common sense.

I see that you are judging me and I do not appreciate it. The thing is, a person like you can't for the life of you understand a person like me. The way I feel, on the inside. The way I grew up. The things I understand. The things I understand aren't things that you could possibly understand. For one thing, you have already told me that you don't believe in God.

But I do. And that is why there will always be a divide between us, why I don't think it's worth my time to talk about the things that are important to me with you. You don't know — you don't want to know — what a terrible time this has been until our President was elected, and the kind of hope that we have now. The hope that we thought was gone for good. You must see that a person cannot be humiliated forever. A person won't put up with it. I won't put up with it. And now I feel as if I am being respected.

Sisterhood, whatever, that's just something your type says. You don't understand real sisterhood, between me and my family and my friends. Really trusting someone, really being able to depend on someone. Really loving someone. And what that has to do with this woman who I believe wholly in my heart is a liar, what that has to do with her is nothing. She is — I don't know. Maybe someone hurt her, but that has nothing to do with Judge Kavanaugh, who as far as I can tell is a good person and always has been. You saw that way his wife was sitting behind him, with her sad face. You saw that way she supported him. And that's the truth that I believe in — why should I believe that other woman, and not his wife?

You couldn't possibly understand.

Score plays.

ANONYMOUS 1 offers to shake hands with SUSAN COLLINS. They shake hands. ANONYMOUS 1 offers her hand to ANONYMOUS 2, who shakes it. ANONYMOUS 1 offers her hand to ANONYMOUS 3 and ANONYMOUS 4, who refuse it. ANONYMOUS 1 offers her hand to MARIA GALLAGER and ANA MARIA ARCHILA, who refuse it. ANONYMOUS 1 offers her hand to JEFF FLAKE, who shakes it. ANONYMOUS 1 takes her chair and exits, stage left.

SCENE FIVE

MARIA GALLAGHER and ANA MARIA ARCHILA stand up from their chairs and face JEFF FLAKE.

Score stops.

ARCHILA

(to JEFF FLAKE)

I recognized in Dr. Ford's story that she is telling the truth. What you are doing is allowing someone who actually violated a woman to sit on the Supreme Court. This is not tolerable. You have children in your family. Think about them. I have two children.[9]

GALLAGHER

(to JEFF FLAKE)

I was sexually assaulted and nobody believed me. I didn't tell anyone, and you're telling all women that they don't matter, that they should just stay quiet because if they tell you what happened to them you are going to ignore them. That's what happened to me, and that's what you are telling all women in America, that they don't matter … That's what you're telling all of these women. That's what you're telling me right now. Look at me when I'm talking to you. You are telling me that my assault doesn't matter, that what happened to me doesn't, and that you're going to let people who do these things into power. That's what you're telling me when you vote for him. Don't look away from me.

---

9   This text is taking from the statements of two protesters who confronted Jeff Flake (R-AZ) on September 28, 2019, *see* note 6, *supra*. The two protesters are Ana Maria Archila and Maria Gallagher, whose recorded statements were made available on the NEW YORK TIMES website. The video is sometimes imperfectly shot, and I have attempted to give the correct attribution to the speakers.

SENATOR JEFF FLAKE stands up from his chair and faces the audience.

SUSAN COLLINS

The Senator from Arizona, Senator Flake.

FLAKE

I think it would be proper to delay the floor vote for up to but not more than one week —[10]

GALLAGHER

Look at me and tell me that it doesn't matter what happened to me, that you will let people like that go into the highest court of the land and tell everyone what they can do to their bodies.

FLAKE

— it would be proper to delay the floor vote for up to but not more than one week in order to let the FBI do an investigation, limited in time and scope to the current allegations that are there.

ARCHILA

Do you think that he's able to hold the pain of this country and repair it?

---

10   This is the text transcribed and adapted from Flake's statements to the Judiciary Committee after his meeting with the protesters and before his vote on September 28, 2108, see THE WASHINGTON POST, *Senate Judiciary Committee Votes On Kavanaugh*, YOUTUBE.COM, Sept. 28, 2018, https://www.youtube.com/watch?v=H7y8SB8Rp1M.

FLAKE

And limited in time to no more than one week. And I will vote
to advance the bill to the floor with that understanding. I have
spoken to a few other members who, on my side of the aisle, are
maybe supportive as well. But that's my position. I think that we
ought to do —

ARCHILA

That is the work of justice. The way that justice works is you
recognize hurt, you take responsibility for it and then you begin
to repair it. You are allowing someone who is unwilling to take
responsibility for his own actions and willing to hold the harm —

FLAKE

The chairman has bent over backwards to do investigations from
this committee and to delay this vote in this committee for a week
so that Judge, or that, uh—

ARCHILA

No. I want to talk to him. Don't talk to me. What do you think? … I
understand, but tell me. I'm standing right here in front of you.

FLAKE

— so that Ms. Ford, that Dr. Ford could be heard. And she was
yesterday. And so with that agreement I'll vote to advance the bill
to the floor.

GALLAGHER

We can't get an answer? There is only one question — being heard
by the highest people in power that they're —

ARCHILA

Do what is right.

FLAKE

Thank you.

Score plays.

*FLAKE offers his hand to ARCHILA and GALLAGHER, who refuse it.
FLAKE offers his hand to ANONYMOUS 2, who shakes it. FLAKE offers
his hand to ANONYMOUS 3 and 4. ANONYMOUS 3 shakes his hand
but ANONYMOUS 4 refuses it. SUSAN COLLINS shakes FLAKE'S hand.
FLAKE picks up his chair and exits, stage right.*

*ARCHILA and GALLAGHER offer their hands to ANONYMOUS 2, who
shakes with them. ARCHILA and GALLAGHER shake hands with
ANONYMOUS 3 and ANONYMOUS 4. ARCHILA and GALLAGHER offer
their hands to SUSAN COLLINS, who refuses them. ARCHILA and
GALLAGHER pick up their chairs and exit, stage left.*

SCENE SIX

ANONYMOUS 2 stands up from his chair and regards the audience.

Score stops.

ANONYMOUS 2

I wonder if I have a helpful perspective. It's weird 'cause I don't know how I feel about it. I have all of these feelings all at once. I feel like because I'm a guy I'm constantly thinking about it in ways that like my wife can't. I think she won't — she has a visceral reaction to it: "They hate women, this stinks, this is a farce." And I feel all those things too, but she has a super visceral reaction to all of it.

My reaction isn't, it's not quite as visceral. Or not in the same way. It's made me think, the one thing that bothered me, I'll tell you about the things that bother me. There are two things. First, when people began to call into question Blasey Ford and Deborah Ramirez and start characterizing the entire thing as a political hit job, or a conspiracy, for me the thing that bothered me was there was no willingness to create a space to hear what happened.

I think that what bothered me is this presumption of bad faith, and that was a conspiracy ginned up by Democrats. It's such a presumption that Democrats will do anything, and that they're the enemy, and that the #MeToo movement is itself like a conspiracy and a sham. It's obscene. It bothers me because it means something bigger. It means that there's no place for people to agree.

One other thing, this might be male perspective. I did kind of grapple with this 'cause I'm also, I'm a guy. I was kind of thinking: How are facts established? What should the standard be? What amount of evidence would I need to kind of believe one thing or another thing? And what if I was ever kind of in a position, what if I'm ever in this position, like, what should the standard be?

And then I feel like that's not something that my wife would think about.

Because this did happen to me once, a long time ago. I broke up with a girlfriend and she didn't like it. She was really mad at me, and then she started saying that I did something to her when we were together, but I did not. I did not do anything to her. She was just mad. See, it's really hard to talk about. But I got called into my college dean's office and there was a procedure, and I didn't do any of it. I'm not saying that women don't tell the truth. I'm just saying that I did not do anything to her. And there was just, like, no process. No process for me. And later, when it was over, and I — nothing happened to me. But when it was over, she called me, and she said, "I just wanted you to know that you couldn't do that to me." And what she meant was that I couldn't break up with her without suffering the consequences, not … So, all I'm saying is, there has to be a process that we can all trust. That we can all believe in. I hope you're not looking at me weird right now. I'm just saying that, if we can't trust each other — I didn't do anything. I'm just saying that if we can't trust each other, everything's lost.

Score plays.

ANONYMOUS 2 offers his hand to ANONYMOUS 3 and 4, who reject it. ANONYMOUS 2 offers his hand to SUSAN COLLINS, who shakes it. ANONYMOUS 2 picks up his chair and exits, stage right.

SCENE SEVEN

ANONYMOUS 3 stands on stage facing the audience. She holds a phone. She holds it up and looks at its screen.

Score stops.

ANONYMOUS 3

(Reading off phone)

"In a final effort to stop Brett Kavanaugh's confirmation, the Women's March and other organizations have announced the Cancel Kavanaugh march … Liberal activists believe they have a shot at convincing Republican senators Susan Collins of Maine, Lisa Murkowski of Alaska, and Jeff Flake of Arizona, along with Democratic senators Heidi Heitkamp of North Dakota and Joe Manchin of West Virginia, to vote no —"[11]

(looks up, pauses for a beat)

I get that women are really upset about this. White women. I mean, I am too. I'm upset. This guy is the worst. I watched him crying, and the privilege. We all know that he assaulted her. We all know that he is a liar. And we *know* this guy. We met this guy in college, knew to stay away from him. And now he's going to be on the Supreme Court.

But I'm not exactly running to the protests. People of color aren't really showing up to the protests. I'm just like watching it on T.V. and feeling like — I haven't exactly been — I'm depressed. The whole thing is making me depressed, but not just because I've been sexually assaulted. Have I been sexually assaulted? Yes.

But they are not me and they will never be me. You can't just make me your representative or proxy because — don't they

11   Victoria Rodriguez, *Women's March Plans #CancelKavanaugh Protest To Sway Senators Before Confirmation Vote*, MASHABLE, Oct. 3, 2018, https://mashable.com/article/womens-march-cancel-kavanaugh/#36pz_SQJwPqg.

realize that when they're getting arrested it's a privilege? My family tried to keep me out of jail my whole life.

And it's like, they're upset *now?* Storming the Senate *now?* Why now? I'll tell you why now. Because it's a White woman. I don't want to offend, I don't mean to diminish — but it's the truth.

Black men and Black women getting killed in the streets every day. I wake up every day, read the paper, and I feel sick. And then I'm seeing all of these false equivalencies: "Oh, now I know what Black people feel like." Or, and this is a good one: "This is worse than what happened to Anita Hill."

No, you do not know what I feel like, and no, this is not worse than what happened to Anita Hill. Everybody making such a deal about how emotional Blasey Ford is and how not emotional Anita Hill was. Well, they don't know emotion when they see it. I know that I am not coming off as sympathetic to this cause. I am. But I'm angry.

Because where were you when we were getting shot in the street by the police? Where were you when Brett Kavanaugh was sitting on the DC circuit and destroying Black people? Why weren't you storming — sorry. I mean, I'm not sorry. It's not shameful to cry. But where were they? Didn't they care? It's like, maybe White women are just interested in us when they're getting disappointed and they need a metaphor.

It's not like I don't feel for her. Blasey Ford. Because I do. I saw her. It was terrible. She was just trying to get through this terrifying experience. But, please, do not say that you know how Black people feel, and you care, and we're here in solidarity. Because really, I think, we're maybe not, or not always.

Score plays.

ANONYMOUS 3 offers her hand to SUSAN COLLINS, who rejects it. She offers her hand to ANONYMOUS 4, who shakes it. ANONYMOUS 3 picks up her chair and exits, stage left.

SCENE EIGHT

SUSAN COLLINS (R-ME) rises from her chair and faces the audience.

Score stops.

ANONYMOUS 4

The Senator from Washington, Senator Collins.

SUSAN COLLINS

Mr. President, one can only hope that the Kavanaugh nomination is where the process has finally hit rock bottom. We hope that the nomination has hit bottom, and it's finally. We hope to hit bottom. We hit bottom hope finally.[12]

I've never considered the president's identity or party when evaluating Supreme Court nominations. Nominations must be considered without considering the president's identity or party. The party or identity should not be evaluated or considered. The nomination should be considered but not the identity evaluated.

I talked with Judge Kavanaugh for more than two hours in my office. For hours we talked in my office about. Two hours I talked with him. And then I talked with him a second time. We talked by phone a second time. We talked on the phone for another hour, we spoke for another hour. We talked on the phone.

In short, his views on honoring precedent would preclude attempts to do by stealth that which one has committed not to do overtly. One should not do by stealth what one can do overtly, and overtly one should not do things by stealth. We should stealthily honor precedent unless we can do it overtly. Overtly we should stealth.

---

12   I have severely altered the text of Susan Collins' October 5, 2018 speech, which can be found at note 7, *supra*.

He noted repeatedly that *Roe* has been upheld by *Planned Parenthood v. Casey*. When I asked him would it be sufficient to overturn a long established precedent if five current Justices believed it was wrongly decided, he emphatically said "no." No. No. No. No. No. No. No. No. No. No. I asked him repeatedly. No. No. No. No. No. No. No. No. No. I asked if five current Justices believed. He emphatically said no.

Mr. President, I listened carefully to Christine Blasey Ford's testimony before the Judiciary Committee. I found her testimony to be sincere, painful, and compelling. I believe that she is a survivor of a sexual assault and that this trauma has upended her life. I listened carefully. Sincerely I listened to the pain and compulsion. I believe that upended the trauma is the sexual assault that I carefully survived.

The allegations fail to meet the more likely than not standard. The more likely a standard is. The standard is more not than likely. Therefore, I do not believe that these charges can fairly prevent Judge Kavanaugh from serving on the court.

Despite the turbulent, bitter fight surrounding his nomination, my fervent hope is that Brett Kavanaugh will work to lessen the divisions in the Supreme Court so that we have far fewer 5-4 decisions and so that public confidence in our Judiciary and our highest court is restored. Bitter is the restoration of Brett Kavanaugh who will work. The division is turbulent and bitter and surrounding. Brett Kavanaugh is restored and we have fewer. Brett Kavanaugh will work to lessen. Bitter is the public confidence of the fervent hope.

Mr. President, I will vote to confirm Judge Kavanaugh.

Score plays.

SUSAN COLLINS offers her hand to ANONYMOUS 4, who rejects it. SUSAN COLLINS picks up her chair and exits, stage left.

SCENE NINE

ANONYMOUS 4 stands up from her chair and faces the audience.

Score stops.

ANONYMOUS 4

(Takes phone out of her pocket, and reads from screen.)

"Brett Kavanaugh was sworn in on Saturday as the 114th Associate Justice of the Supreme Court, after the Senate voted largely along party lines to confirm his nomination amid an emotional, weeks-long debate characterized by explosive allegations of sexual assault."[13]

(looks up)

Some people can't talk about it. About what's happening. But you can't talk about what's happening unless you also talk about the people who can't talk about it. I mean, I can't talk about it.

I can't talk about it. This thing that happened. I can't talk about it because it's not getting better. I mean, it happens to women like me too. I'm White. I'm very privileged. I wasn't so privileged when this happened to me, but, yeah.

It's always there looming in the back of my mind. But it wouldn't cross my mind on an average day, month, week. It doesn't seem to be a force in my life anymore. And then when, you know, the Kavanaugh/Christine Blasey Ford came out, and we knew we would be hearing her testimony, I realized that I was having trouble sleeping. I was nauseated.

Yesterday, Public Radio, they were interviewing someone, she was saying, "I don't know any women who haven't had this

---

13   Kevin Breuninger & Mike Calia, *Brett Kavanaugh Sworn In As Supreme Court Justice After Raucous Debate, Narrow Senate Victory*, CNBC.com, Oct. 6, 2018, https://www.cnbc.com/2018/10/06/brett-kavanaugh-confirmed-by-senate-in-50-48-vote.html.

experience." I heard 40 percent. This past week they were saying 30 percent.

And this is just brought it all up again. No matter how far away we thought it was. It's tough. I can't get out of bed. It's residing in my body. The sleep issues, the nausea, the lack of energy. I can't get anything done. I'm just coasting through, doing the minimum. I'm just walking through the day. It's not — it just feels, I'm just feeling it very physically and for some reason that is surprising me.

Score plays.

ANONYMOUS 4 is alone. There is no one to shake her hand or reject it. She picks up her chair and exits stage right.

Score stops.

END

ADVICE AND CONSENT

SCORE

Preface

THE MUSICAL SCORE to the play *Advice and Consent* includes a total of 10 separate pieces. The pieces are numbered scenes one through nine with a finale. Each numbered piece should be performed at the start of its corresponding scene in the play. The 10th and final part of the score follows scene nine and closes the play.

I composed all sections of the score with the exception of the finale, which I arranged based on Carrie Robinson's performance of *Power to Live Right*, captured on film on Maxwell Street, Chicago, Illinois, in 1964.

Each of the score's 10 sections should be used as lead sheets. The instrumentation and tempo of each section is indicated at the top of the page. The score in its entirety requires nine players, however, only the finale calls for the simultaneous participation of all nine players. Most sections are designed for smaller combinations of players including a solo, duets, trios and quintets. The score encourages improvisation; some sections include a head to be performed by one to two lead instruments; some sections indicate a vamp that can be repeated under rotating solos.

The score includes the following instruments in order of appearance: violin, trumpet, tenor saxophone, contrabass, drums, piano, flute, and two vocals. The finale, which instructs the participation of all players, does not obligate the playing of every instrument. For example, the horns may choose to add percussion, or the violin and flute, may choose to alternate between playing their instruments and adding vocals.

The nine players that comprise the score's ensemble should reflect basic demographic diversity: At least five of the nine players should be women and/or LGBTQ+ and at least four of the nine should be people of color.

SCENE ONE

Solo Violin

SCENE TWO

Trumpet & Tenor Sax

SCENE THREE

Trumpet & Tenor Sax

SCENE FOUR

Violin, Trumpet & Tenor Sax

<u>SCENE FIVE</u>

Bass & Drums

Vamp Out

<u>SCENE SIX</u>

Bass, Drums & Keys

Vamp Out

SCENE SEVEN

Bass, Drums, Keys & Horns

SCENE EIGHT

Bass, Drums, Keys, Flute & Violin

SCENE NINE

Flute Violin and Bass

FINALE

Arrangement Inspired by Carrie Robinson's *Power to Live Righ.*

Full Ensemble: All Players + Vocals

END

Yxta Maya Murray is a writer and a professor at Loyola Law School in Los Angeles.

She would like to thank her interviewees, Allan Ides, Kathleen Kim, Tom Lutz, Boris Dralyuk, Ellie Duke, Stephanie Malak, and Andrew Brown. She is grateful and indebted to the work of Anna Deavere Smith, Lynn Nottage, Ntozake Shange, and Luis Valdez.

Kathleen Kim is professor of law at Loyola Law School in Los Angeles. She is also an experimental musician and composer.

She would like to thank the *Los Angeles Review of Books*, Tim Eastman, LA Fog, and Loyola Law School.

CPSIA information can be obtained
at www.ICGtesting.com
Printed in the USA
LVHW091910280219
609127LV00004B/4/P